Designed and packaged by
Q2A Creative
Printed in India

C O N T E N T S

THE CELTS AND ROMANS

EARLY settlers in what is now England, were called Celts. They are believed to have come to England from other parts of Europe over 2,000 years ago. Whatever information we have about the Celts was obtained mainly from the Greeks and Romans, Wales, Scotland, Ireland and the Isle of Man are now predomiantly populated by Celts.

Queen Boudicca was one of the best known Celtic warriors. She was the chief of the Iceni tribe and led the rebellion against the invading Romans

A Celtic chieftain fully armoured

First farmers

The Celts lived in tribes and each tribe was led by a chieftain. Since the primary source of living was agriculture, the Celts spent most of their time farming and rearing cattle and horses. However, some of them were also trained soldiers.

Celtic life

The Celts lived in round-houses of mud and straw. However, the chieftain, soldiers and other important people lived in hill-forts, mainly since these were easier to defend against rival tribes. It is likely that class divisions existed among the Celts. This was evident in their clothes too. Men wore trousers, tunics and cloaks, while women wore dresses adorned with brooches. Important individuals, including the king, wore torcs around their necks.

Warriors on call

The various Celtic tribes were believed to have fought among themselves. Hence, every tribe member had to learn the art of warfare and took part in battles whenever the tribal chieftain called on them. Even women entered the battlefield when it was required. Swords and spears were the main Celtic weapons. They also used horse-drawn chariots.

Celtic legends talk about a king named Arthur who proved his right to the throne of England after he drew the sword of Excalibur from a rock

FACT BOX

After they conquered England, the Romans set about building towns. One of these, Londinium, became the main port city of the Romans. It stood at the site of modern-day London. In AD 61, Queen Boudicca burnt the city down and killed several residents. After this, the Romans built a wall around the city to protect it from similar attacks in the future.

Roman invasion

In AD 43 the Romans, led by commander Aulus Plautius, invaded England. After establishing their supremacy, the Romans set about building roads, towns, baths and ports. Trade and commerce flourished, opening up England to the world. Although certain Celtic tribes, like the Iceni, continued to resist the Romans, most of them adapted to the Roman way of life. The relationship between Celts and Romans improved gradually.

The Iceni tribe continued to resist the Romans.

CELTIC TIMELINE

c. 8300 BC
Hunter-gatherers arrive in England
6300-5500 BC
Farming develops
c. 1800 BC
Roundhouses appear
c. 500 BC
The Iron Age begins in England
55-54 BC
Roman emperor Julius Caesar attempts to invade England
AD 43
Romans invade England
AD 410
Romans abandon England

ANGLO-SAXONS AND VIKINGS

THE decline of the Roman Empire encouraged barbaric tribes like the Visigoths to invade Rome. The Romans needed their entire army to defend their homeland. Thus, about 400 years after they first came to England, the Roman forces withdrew. England became weak and defenceless, and soon fell prey to invasions by the Anglo-Saxons and Vikings.

Map of England during Anglo -Saxon rule. It comprised five main kingdoms

✠ Anglo-Saxon invasion

The Anglo-Saxon invaders belonged to the Angle, Saxon and Jute tribes. They sailed from Germany, Denmark and Holland in wooden boats. By AD 600, these tribes had occupied most of England and set up their own kingdoms. The five main kingdoms were Northumbria, Mercia, Wessex, Kent and East Anglia.

✠ Ethelbert of Kent

The famous Anglo-Saxon kings included Ethelbert of Kent, Offa and Alfred the Great. Ethelbert was the first English king to be converted to Christianity. It was during his reign that Pope Gregory I sent a missionary of about 40 monks, led by St Augustine, to England.

The English silver penny was introduced during Offa's reign

✠ Alfred the Great and the Vikings

Towards the end of the 8th century, the Vikings from Denmark and Norway invaded England. By AD 878, they defeated the Anglo-Saxons and conquered most of their kingdoms, except Wessex, which was ruled by Alfred the Great. During King Alfred's reign, the Vikings were restricted to northern and eastern England – a region that came to be called Danelaw. This situation continued until AD 978, when King Alfred's descendant, Ethelred II, ascended the throne. The people were so unhappy with Ethelred that they readily accepted Sweyn I, the Danish king, as their new ruler.

As well as for his successful defence of England against Viking conquests, Alfred the Great was also noted for his patronage of learning. He translated several Latin books into English

✠ End of Viking rule

Following Sweyn's death in 1014, Ethelred's son Edmund Ironside took control of Danelaw. However, he was defeated by Sweyn's son, Canute, who allowed Edmund to keep control of Wessex. Canute became the king of England in 1016, after Edmund died. Anglo-Saxon rule returned briefly in 1042, when Ethelred's son, Edward the Confessor, came to power.

The Vikings had ships for various purposes – the knorr to carry goods and the longship for travel and invasions. They also buried their dead kings in ships, along with their weapons, food and finery. Dogs, horses and even humans were sacrificed and buried to keep the dead king company!

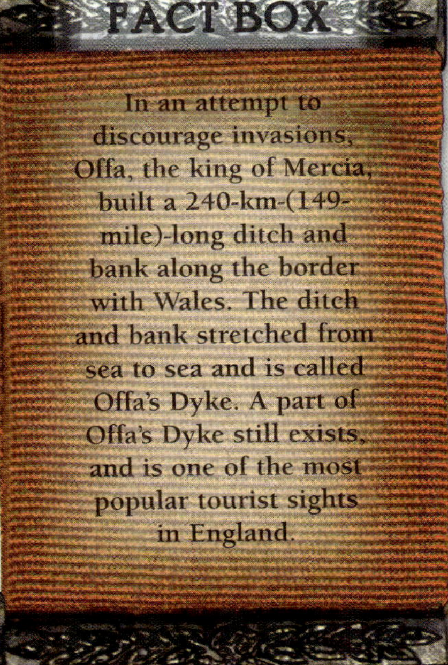

FACT BOX

In an attempt to discourage invasions, Offa, the king of Mercia, built a 240-km-(149-mile)-long ditch and bank along the border with Wales. The ditch and bank stretched from sea to sea and is called Offa's Dyke. A part of Offa's Dyke still exists, and is one of the most popular tourist sights in England.

MAJOR ANGLO-SAXON KINGS' REIGN

Offa: 757-796
Egbert: 802-839
Ethelbald: 856-860
Ethelbert: 860-866
Ethelred I: 866-871
Alfred the Great: 871-899
Edward the Confessor: 1042-1066

VIKING MONARCHS IN ENGLAND

Sweyn I: 1013-1014
Canute the Great: 1016-1035
Harold I: 1035-1040
Hardicanute: 1040-1042

NORMAN ENGLAND

THE death of Edward the Confessor marked the end of both Anglo-Saxon and Viking rule in England. There was no one from either dynasty who could claim the throne. This led to a power struggle leading to the Norman Conquest.

Edward and the Normans

Edward's attachment with the nobility from Normandy, France, made him unpopular with one of the most powerful earls of the time, Godwin of Wessex. Although Edward was married to the earl's daughter, Godwin rebelled. Edward banished him from England and continued to support the Normans. It is believed that Edward, during this period, chose William of Normandy as his successor.

The construction of the Tower of London was begun by William the Conqueror as a series of fortifications

William the Conqueror

A few years later, Edward formed a close friendship with Godwin's son, Harold. It is said that the king named Harold his heir before he died. William, duke of Normandy, on the other side, insisted that Edward had named him heir in 1051. William also asserted that Harold had vowed not to lay his claim When Harold was crowned in 1066, William invaded England. The ensuing Battle of Hastings ended with Harold's death.

During the Battle of Hastings, rumours regarding William's death spread among his soldiers, who began to retreat. William took off his helmet and rode through the battlefield to reassure his army

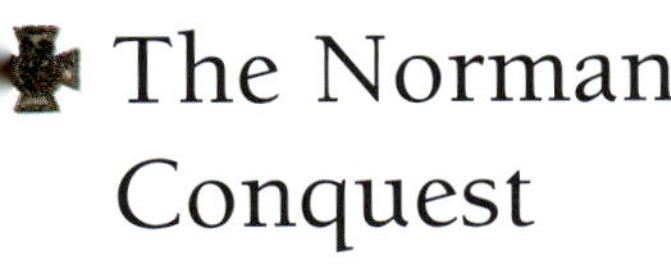
The Norman Conquest

The English nobility was not ready to accept William as king. Instead, they put Edgar, the 13-year-old great-grandson of Ethelred II, on the throne. However, they finally gave in and William was crowned king. William's invasion is known as the Norman Conquest.

William the Conqueror was regarded as one of the greatest soldiers of the Middle Ages

Succession among the Normans was contentious. After William I, his eldest son Robert became the duke of Normandy, while the younger son, William II, was crowned king of England. William II was succeeded by his younger brother Henry. Later, Henry imprisoned Robert and became the duke. Upon Henry's death, his nephew, Stephen, succeeded him instead of Henry's daughter Matilda.

Norman reformations

Norman influence on England is evident in almost all aspects, from social structure to architecture. One of the most notable achievements of the time was the Domesday Book – a survey conducted on property ownership. Several churches and castles, including the Ely Cathedral, were also built during this period. Windsor Castle was built by William the Conqueror as a fortress.

NORMAN KINGS' REIGN

William the Conqueror
1066-1087
William II
1087-1100
Henry I
1100-1135
Stephen
1135-1154

Windsor Castle was originally made of wood. It was only during the 12th century that the wooden structure was replaced with stones

SERVING ROYALTY

THE Norman rule witnessed a change not just in the political system of England, but also in the social structure of the time. It was during this era that the feudal system became prominent. The feudal way of life continued in England for most of the Middle Ages.

It was William I who introduced knights to the English armed forces. Knights usually fought on horses, but were also trained to fight on foot

The feudal pyramid – a reflection of the political, economic and social structure in Europe during the Middle Ages

✠ Feudal pyramid

In the feudal system, the king made land grants to his nobles and promised to protect them. The nobles, in return, promised their loyalty and a supply of soldiers to the royal army. Poor people and peasants worked on the lands of the nobles, who provided them with protection. The poor people, called serfs, became tenants of the lords for life.

✠ Knights

The lords also maintained a unit of cavalry to protect their interests. However, horses were so expensive that even the rich could not afford them. So, the lords decided to make horse owners their tenants. This way, the lords did not have to keep their own horses and stables. From this system arose a new class of people – the knights.

Feudal England

The feudal system existed in England
even earlier. However, it was
William I who brought everybody
into its fold. Under this system, the
king became sole owner of a huge
portion of land. William seized the
lands of several earls, replacing
them with Norman barons. He
also created more than 150
'honours', which were lands in
shires governed by knights.
The barons also created
knights, thus forming
private armies.

During William's reign, castles were seats of administration. Several castles were built in the shires, and lords were responsible for governing the lands in the area

The Church

Being a devout Christian, William I made the church stronger.
Several acres of land were given to the church. Most bishops
and abbots became the king's tenants-in-chief. William relied
heavily on his bishops to make administrative decisions.
In fact, Lanfranc, the archbishop of Canterbury, helped
in the administration of England during William's
absence. The archbishop also reorganised the
Church of England, and even set up church
courts to deal with religious matters.

The present Rochester Cathedral dates back to Norman England. Work on the building was begun by Gundulf, the then bishop of Rochester and also chief castle builder for William I, in 1077

FEUDAL SYSTEM IN ENGLAND

The king
Owned the lands,
which he divided into fiefs
Tenants-in-chief
Barons and earls
who governed the fiefs
Sub-tenants
Knights created by
the barons and earls
Villeins
Peasants who worked the lands

THE ANGEVIN DYNASTY

THE Angevin Dynasty refers to the descendants of the count of Anjou, a French province. King Henry II was the first Angevin to ascend the throne of England. He was followed by Richard I and John.

The coat of arms of the Angevin Dynasty

Stephen and Matilda

Before his death, King Henry I had named his daughter Matilda as his successor. However, the English nobility refused to accept a woman as their ruler. They favoured Henry's nephew, Stephen. Matilda was married to Geoffrey Plantagenet, the count of Anjou at the time. Matilda invaded England, but did not succeed in capturing the throne. Few years later, her son Henry set out to claim the English throne.

As the third son of King Henry II, Richard was in the beginning an unlikely contender to the throne of England

King Henry II

To discourage Henry, Stephen nominated his son Eustace as heir. However, Eustace died in 1153 and Stephen finally named Henry his successor. Henry's attempts to take control of his wife, Eleanor's, lands led to confrontations between him and his children, particularly Richard, who was Eleanor's heir. Henry II died in 1189, soon after being defeated by an alliance between Richard and King Philip II of France. That same year, Richard became king.

During the reign of the Angevins, the Parliament became strong and powerful

Richard the Lion-heart

King Richard I spent only six months of his 10-year reign in his new kingdom. Soon after his coronation, the new king joined the Third Crusade, a holy war against Saladin, an Islamic warrior. Richard's success during the crusade earned him the name of 'Lion-heart'. He meant to return to England after signing a peace treaty with Saladin at Jaffa. On the way, though, he was taken captive by the German emperor Henry VI, to be released only after a year for a huge ransom amount. Following his return in 1194, Richard was re-crowned king. However, he died in a minor battle against a baron five years later.

King John and the Magna Carta

Upon Richard's death, his brother John became king of England. John soon lost Normandy and Anjou to Philip II, and spent the rest of his reign trying to recover these territories. His tax reforms were resented and he was also excommunicated by the Pope. In June 1215, a group of dissatisfied barons forced the king to sign the Magna Carta – a peace treaty that limited the king's powers and upheld the freedom and rights of his subjects.

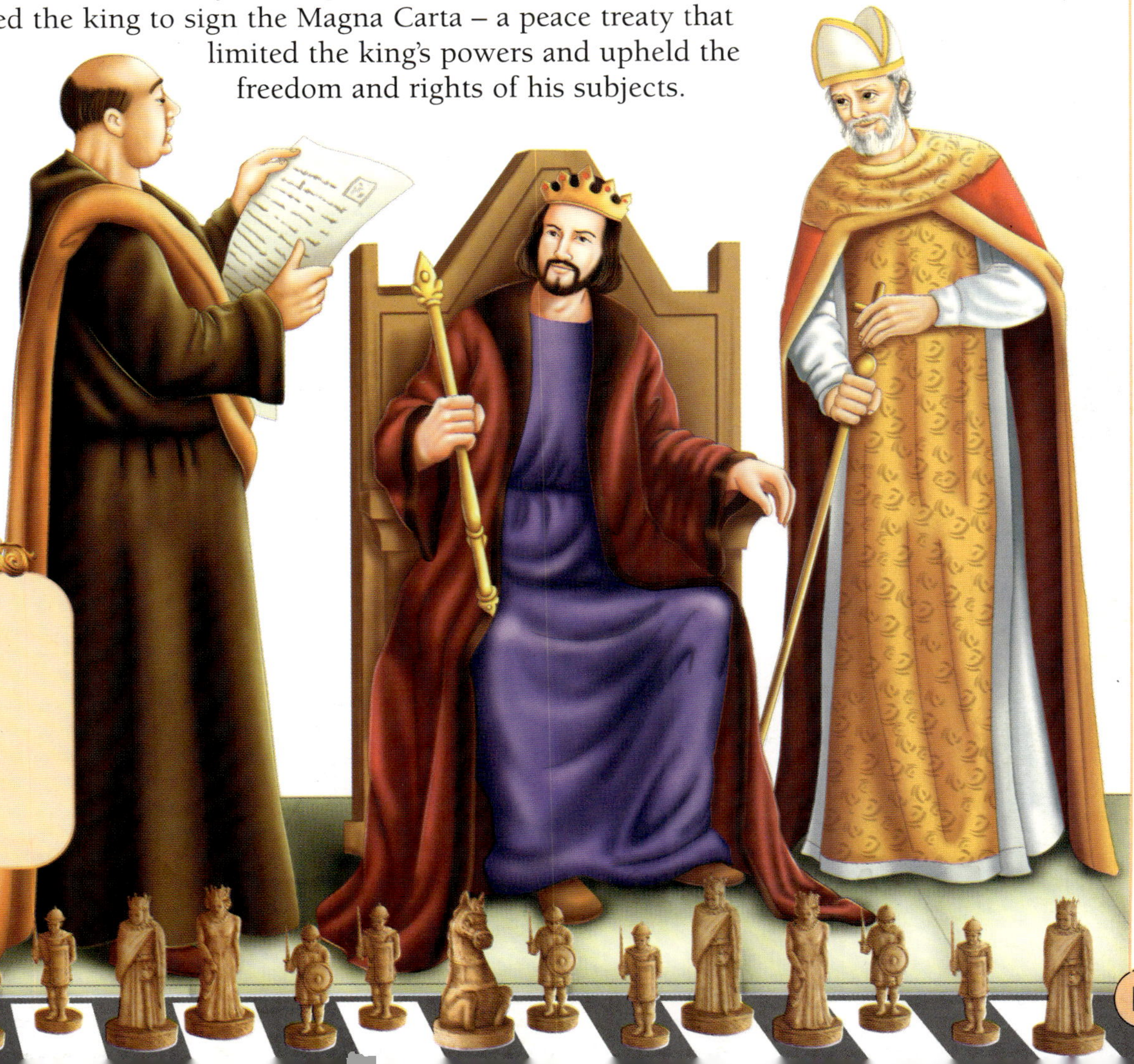

The legendary Robin Hood was supposed to have lived during the reign of Richard I. Robin Hood was a hero who stole from the rich and gave to the poor. In the story, King John was portrayed as the bad king who troubled Robin, while Richard was the good king who returned after the wars and pardoned the outlaw.

Although King John signed the Magna Carta, he did not abide by it. A baronial uprising and civil war was only averted by the king's death

THE ANGEVIN MONARCHS' REIGN

Henry II
1154-1189
Richard I
1189-1199
John
1199-1216

THE PLANTAGENET MONARCHS

PLANTAGENET was the nickname of Matilda's husband Geoffrey of Anjou. It was derived from the broom flower that the count had adapted as his emblem. Some historians regard his son Henry II as the first of the Plantagenet line of kings. Others identify Henry III, son of King John II, as the first Plantagenet.

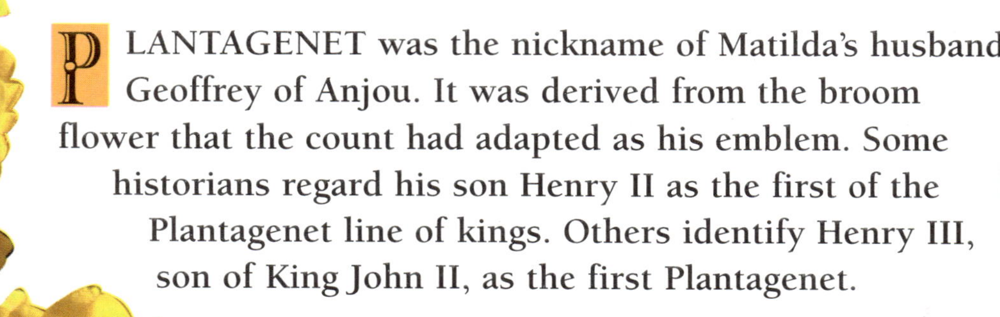

The broom flower that gave its name to the Plantagenet monarchs

After Ethelred in 1013, Edward II was the first monarch to be dethroned

Scotland and Wales

Among the most significant events during the Plantagenet rule were the capture of Wales and the invasion of Scotland. Edward I, the son of King Henry III, conquered Wales and made his son, Edward II, the Prince of Wales. He then attacked Scotland. However, the Scots, led by William Wallace and later by Robert the Bruce, could not be defeated.

Initially Robert the Bruce, king of Scotland, supported Edward I and swore loyalty to the English king in 1296. However, his sense of patriotism got the better of Bruce and hardly a year later, he joined the Scottish revolt

Edward II

Edward II was the most unpopular of the Plantagenet monarchs. His reign was marked by power struggles between the king and the barons. He also lost a major battle against the Scots in 1314. In 1326 Edward's wife, Isabella of France, rebelled against him. Finally, in 1327, Isabella and her allies captured the king and forced him to give up the throne in favour of his son, Edward III.

The Hundred Years' War

Edward III was the most significant of all the Plantagenet monarchs. He was the nephew of Charles IV of France. Since Charles had no son, Edward was the natural heir to the throne of France. However, the French nobles did not want Edward as their king and crowned his cousin, Philip VI, instead. This led to the famous Hundred Years' War between the two countries.

King Edward III conferring the knighthood.
In 1348, Edward founded the Order of the Garter, the oldest order of knighthood in Britain as well as one of the most distinguished

The Hundred Years' War between England and France actually lasted for 116 years. Beginning in 1337, the conflict ended in 1453 with the Battle of Castillon. The battles, separated by periods of truce, were mainly fought in France. The English kings who saw through the war were Edward III, Richard II, Henry IV, Henry V and Henry VI.

PLANTAGENET MONARCHS' REIGN

Henry III
1216-1272
Edward I 'Longshanks'
1272-1307
Edward II
1307-1327
Edward III
1327-1377
Richard II
1377-1399

Peasants' Revolt

In 1377, Parliament imposed poll taxes to meet the cost of the war against France. The peasants, already unhappy with their wages, called for a fixed rent for land and also demanded abolition of the system of serfs. Richard II, the 14-year-old grandson of Edward III, agreed to meet the demands. However, following the killing of rebel leaders Wat Tyler and John Ball, the king refused to keep his promises and, in this manner, the Peasants' Revolt of 1381 failed.

WARS OF THE ROSES

THE end of the reign of King Richard II marked the beginning of one of the most prominent power struggles in England's history. The conflict occurred between the royal Houses of Lancaster and York.

The red rose of the House of Lancaster

Henry IV

The eldest son of Edward III died before his father. So, when the king died, his grandson Richard II succeeded him. Several nobles, including his cousin Henry Bolingbroke, opposed Richard's crowning. Henry was the son of John of Gaunt, who was the duke of Lancaster and the third son of Edward III. When John died, Richard banished Henry from the country. However, Richard's unpopularity helped Henry to eventually oust his cousin. He assumed the kingship as Henry IV.

The others in line

Other claimants to the crown included descendants of Lionel of Antwerp, the second son of Edward III. Lionel had only one child, a daughter named Philippa. She married Edmund Mortimer, the 3rd earl of March. They had a son named Roger, whom Richard II named as heir. Roger died in 1398, leaving his son Edmund Mortimer to succeed him. However, Henry Bolingbroke sidestepped Edmund's claims to the throne.

The dynastic civil war between the Lancastrians and Yorkists was marked by a series of bloody battles. The first of these took place at St Albans (May 22, 1455) in England, and ended in a Yorkist victory

House of York

The House of York was founded by Edmund of Langley, the fourth son of Edward III. Edmund was also the first duke of York. His sons were Edward, duke of York, and Richard, earl of Cambridge. Richard was executed for plotting against King Henry V and trying to claim the throne for his brother-in-law, Edmund Mortimer.

The white rose represented the House of York

The name 'Wars of the Roses' has its origins in the badges of the two royal houses involved in the conflict. The House of Lancaster had adopted a red rose as its badge, while a white rose represented the House of York. Both houses asserted their claims to the throne of England, by virtue of being descendants of King Edward III.

The showdown

The actual Wars of the Roses began during the reign of Henry VI, son of Henry V. The new Lancastrian king's inefficient governance encouraged Richard, the duke of York and the son of Richard, earl of Cambridge, to stake claim to the throne. However, the duke died in 1460 at the Battle of Wakefield. His eldest son, Edward, successfully pursued the claim and was crowned King Edward IV of England in 1461.

THE LANCASTRIANS' REIGN

Henry IV
1399-1413
Henry V
1413-1422
Henry VI
1422-1461, 1470-1471

THE YORKISTS' REIGN

Edward IV
1461-1470, 1471-1483
Edward V
April-June 1483
Richard III
1483-1485

In 1461, King Henry VI was deposed by Edward of York. Later, Henry was imprisoned in the Tower of London, where he was killed in May 1471

TUDOR ENGLAND

HENRY Tudor defeated King Richard III, the younger brother of King Edward IV, to establish the Tudor dynasty. This dynasty lasted more than a hundred years.

King Richard III

King Edward IV had two sons – Edward and Richard. After the king's sudden death, his younger brother Richard imprisoned the two princes in the Tower of London, and claimed the throne for himself. It is believed that Richard had his nephews killed and buried in the tower.

Rise of the Tudors

Richard III was not very popular among his people. When Henry Tudor challenged him at Bosworth Field in 1485, not many people rushed to the king's side. Henry won the battle and captured the throne. According to a legend, one of Richard's supporters deserted him at the last moment and after the king was killed in the battle, he took the crown and placed it on Henry's head.

Richard III was the last monarch from the House of York

The reign of Henry VII was marked by several revolts. Some of these involved impersonators such as Lambert Simnel and Perkin Warbeck, who were presented as either Edward V or his brother. To protect himself from such plots, the king created personal bodyguards known as Yeomen of the Guard. This is the oldest military corps that exists today.

Henry VII

Henry Tudor was the great-grandson of John of Gaunt, son of King Edward III. A few years before he died, John married his mistress Katherine Swynford. They had four children – John, Henry, Thomas and Joan – all given the surname Beaufort. The Beauforts were actually barred from inheriting the throne. John Beaufort's daughter Margaret married into the House of Tudor. Henry VII was born to Margaret and her husband Edmund.

Elizabeth of York was the model for the 'queen' in the pack of playing cards

**THE TUDOR DYNASTY'
REIGN**

Henry VII
1485-1509
Henry VIII
1509-1547
Edward VI
1547-1553
Mary I
1553-1558
Elizabeth I
1558-1603

The war ends

After he was crowned king of England, Henry VII set about making his position stronger. He realised that being a Lancastrian he was still under threat from the Yorkists. In order to put an end to the feud, the king married Elizabeth of York, the eldest daughter of Edward IV. This united the Houses of Lancaster and York, putting an end to the Wars of the Roses.

The Yeomen of the Guard continue to wear the Tudor uniform of red and gold, and carry halberds

HENRY VIII

KING Henry VIII is one of the best-known English monarchs of all time. The second ruler of the Tudor dynasty, he was famous for his reforms as well as for his many marriages.

After Queen Jane's death, Henry went on to marry three more times – to Anne of Cleves, Katherine Howard and Catherine Parr. None of them had children

✠ The accession

Henry VII had seven children – Arthur, Margaret, Henry, Elizabeth, Mary, Edmund and Katherine. Young Henry was a very intelligent and athletic boy. He was fluent in French, Latin and Spanish. He also wrote books and composed music. When his elder brother Arthur died, Henry became heir to the throne.

✠ The six wives of Henry VIII

King Henry's first wife was Catherine of Aragon. However, since the queen could not produce a male heir, Henry divorced her and married Anne Boleyn. When Queen Anne also failed to give birth to a son, Henry had her killed on charges of treason. He then married Jane Seymour. Jane died after giving birth to Henry's only male heir, Edward. Henry went on to marry three more times, but had no more children.

Anne Boleyn being beheaded. There is a popular rhyme that describes the fate of King Henry's six wives: "Divorced, beheaded, died, divorced, beheaded, survived!"

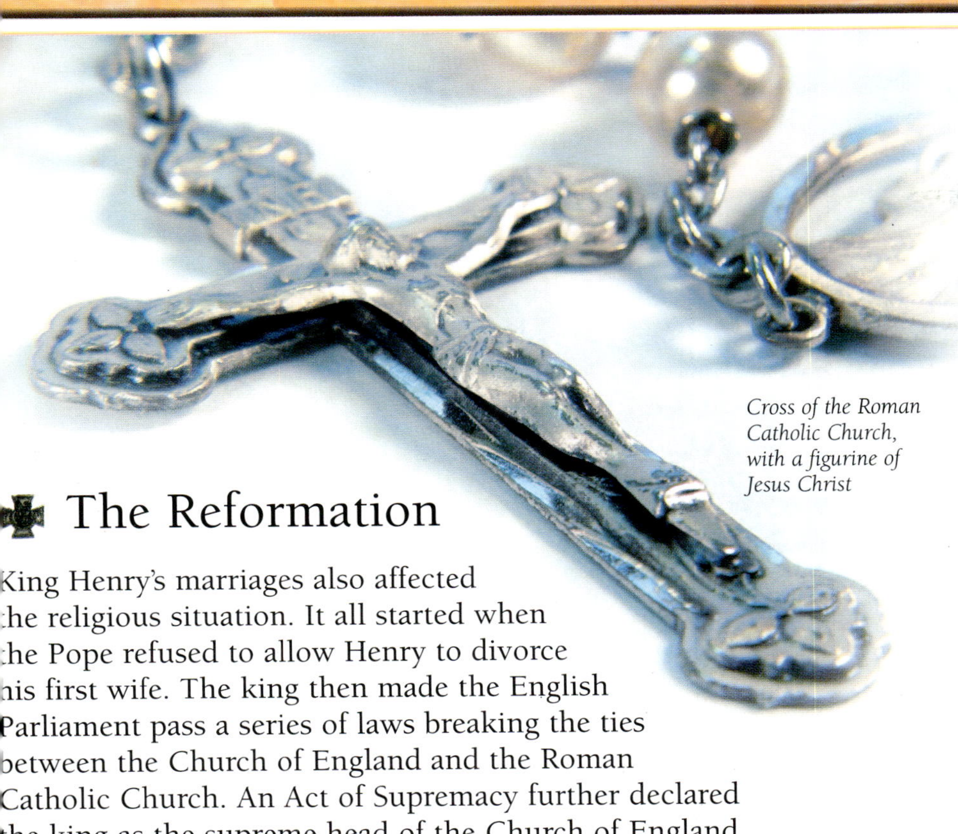

Cross of the Roman Catholic Church, with a figurine of Jesus Christ

The Reformation

King Henry's marriages also affected the religious situation. It all started when the Pope refused to allow Henry to divorce his first wife. The king then made the English Parliament pass a series of laws breaking the ties between the Church of England and the Roman Catholic Church. An Act of Supremacy further declared the king as the supreme head of the Church of England.

Succession

Henry resorted to extreme measures only to have a male heir. He knew that England was not yet ready to accept a female ruler. He was also aware that his only son, Edward, was physically unfit for the job. Eventually, his sixth wife Catherine Parr brought the king and his daughters from his first two marriages, Mary and Elizabeth, together. Henry named them his successors after Prince Edward.

One of the most significant events that occurred during the reign of Henry VIII was the union of England and Wales. This was done through a series of parliamentary acts, now termed Acts of Union (1536-1543). These acts brought Wales under the same laws and administration as England.

HENRY VIII

Born
June 28, 1491
Father
King Henry VII
Mother
Elizabeth of York
Sisters
Margaret, Elizabeth, Mary and Katherine
Brothers
Arthur and Edmund

This armour was especially made for Henry VIII, to be worn at a friendly tournament called Field of Cloth of Gold. Henry was pitted against the French king Francis I. Made at the royal armour workshop at Greenwich Palace, Henry's armour encased the whole body and had no gaps

THE VIRGIN QUEEN

QUEEN Elizabeth I was the last of the Tudor monarchs. Often referred to as the Virgin Queen, Elizabeth ascended the throne of England amidst a lot of difficulties.

Queen Mary I was 37 years old when she ascended the throne. She was the first crowned queen of England

Queen Elizabeth's reign saw England becoming a major European power

SUCCESSORS OF HENRY VIII

Edward VI
(October 12, 1537-July 6, 1553)
Mother – Jane Seymour

Mary I
(February 18, 1516-
November 17, 1558)
Mother – Catherine of Aragon

Elizabeth I
(Sept 7, 1533-March 24, 1603)
Mother – Anne Boleyn

✠ Edward VI

Elizabeth's half-brother and half-sister ruled England before her. King Henry VIII died in 1547, leaving nine-year-old Prince Edward to succeed him. Edward, however, died when he was barely 16 years old, reportedly of tuberculosis.

✠ Queen Mary I

Before dying, Edward named Lady Jane Grey as his successor. Jane was the granddaughter of Mary Tudor, the sister of Henry VIII. However, the people of England wanted Princess Mary, Henry's daughter by Catherine of Aragon, to ascend the throne. Hence, just nine days after she became queen, Lady Jane was replaced by Mary.

✠ Elizabeth's accession

Upon becoming queen, Mary I set about reviving Roman Catholicism in England. In the process, she took several stern decisions. One of them was the execution of Protestant leaders. These steps, combined with her marriage to King Philip II of Spain, made her unpopular. So, when Mary died childless in 1558, the people of England gladly accepted Elizabeth as their new ruler.

During her five-year reign, Queen Mary I ruthlessly proceeded to revert England to Catholicism. In the process, the queen had about 300 Protestants burnt at the stake for heresy. This terrible act earned her the name Bloody Mary. The famous minister John Rogers was the first Protestant to be killed during the time.

After marrying Mary I in 1554, King Philip II of Spain became co-ruler of England until the queen's death

Several attempts by Catholic leaders to place Mary, Queen of Scots, on the throne of England eventually resulted in her trial and final execution

✠ Long live the queen!

Elizabeth was very popular among her people. This made her the target of several murderous plots developed by Catholic leaders who did not want a Protestant queen. Her main rival was Mary Stuart, the Catholic queen of the Scots. Most plots were aimed at replacing Elizabeth with Mary. One such major attempt was the Babington Plot. It is named after Sir Anthony Babington, the chief conspirator. The plan was to kill the queen and crown Mary, who was Elizabeth's prisoner at the time. However, the plot was discovered in time and the queen's life was saved. When Elizabeth found out that Mary was involved in the plot, she had her killed in 1587.

ELIZABETHAN ENGLAND

ELIZABETH'S reign is said to have been the Golden Age of English history. Such famous people as William Shakespeare, Sir Walter Raleigh and Francis Drake lived during her time. Her reign also witnessed several wars that made England more powerful.

The Spanish Armada was defeated at the Battle of Gravelines

The legend goes that Sir Walter Raleigh, renowned English explorer and writer, once took off his cloak and placed it on a puddle, so that Queen Elizabeth could walk across it without soiling her feet

Spanish Armada

During the Elizabethan Era, relations with Spain were very tense as Queen Mary's husband, Philip II of Spain believed that he had a right to the English throne. After Mary's death in 1558, he tried to marry Elizabeth to retain control over England. However, when the queen rejected him, Philip II encouraged plots to kill her. Finally, he had to start planning an invasion. In July 1588, the king sent the Spanish Armada to invade England. The fleet of about 130 ships were considered to be unbeatable. But the English fleet commanded by Francis Drake destroyed the Armada.

Warring times

Philip continued to wage war against England. Meanwhile, the English were busy colonising North America. Walter Raleigh and Humphrey Gilbert led voyages to the New World and encouraged English settlements there. The queen also set up the British East India Company to expand trade relationships with new lands.

Among the several stately homes built during Elizabeth's time, one of the most popular was Longleat House in Wiltshire

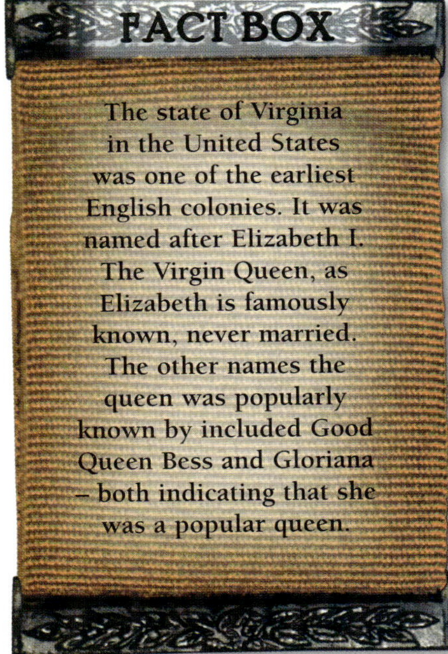

Economy

Despite English victories in various conflicts and the expansion of the empire, things were not going well for Elizabeth at home. The war with Spain had weakened the economy. It is believed that during Elizabeth's reign over five million pounds were spent on wars alone. People living in the countryside had to struggle due to high prices. This led to a decline in the queen's popularity.

Art and culture

Elizabeth's rule proved to be the 'golden age' for English art and literature. Being well-read and talented, the queen encouraged the artists and writers of her time. The theatre flourished and playwrights such as William Shakespeare were especially favoured by the queen. In fact, Elizabeth attended the first staging of Shakespeare's famous comedy, *A Midsummer Night's Dream.*

It is believed that Queen Elizabeth liked Shakespeare's plays and gave him complete support. However, Shakespeare produced his best works much after her death

Accession
1558
Coronation
January 15, 1559
Chief adviser to the queen
William Cecil,
1st Baron Burghley
Chief spy of the queen
Sir Francis Walsingham
Famous explorers during the Elizabethan Era
Sir Francis Drake, Sir Walter Raleigh, Sir Humphrey Gilbert
Famous writers from the era
William Shakespeare, Christopher Marlowe, Ben Jonson

THE STUARTS

IN his will, Henry VIII had said that the descendants of his younger sister, Mary Tudor, would succeed Elizabeth. However, it was Henry's elder sister Margaret's descendants who finally came to power. Margaret had married thrice, each time to a member of the House of Stuart – the rulers of Scotland. Thus it was that the Stuart era finally began in England.

James I

A few hours after Elizabeth's death, King James VI of Scotland was proclaimed king of England and Ireland, as James I. He was the first king to rule all three kingdoms at the same time. A popular legend says that Elizabeth felt guilty about having his mother, Mary, Queen of Scots, killed, and hence named James as heir on her deathbed.

Guy Fawkes was executed opposite the Parliament building that he meant to blow up with his infamous Gunpowder Plot

Gunpowder Plot

James' anti-Catholic policies made him extremely unpopular among the Catholics in England. This led to several attempts to kill him. The most well-known was the Gunpowder Plot of 1605. A group of Catholic rebels led by Guy Fawkes planned to blow up Parliament, when the king and the members of the two houses gathered for the opening session. The plan was discovered, though, and Guy Fawkes was put to death.

✠ James and Parliament

As king of England, James I kept getting into disputes with Parliament. He spent huge amounts of money from the royal treasury. Parliament was not happy about this. It refused to increase taxes simply to meet the king's expenses. Following several such differences, the furious king finally dissolved Parliament in 1611.

King James I at a printing press overseeing the printing of the King James Version of the Bible, the English translation that was first published in 1611

In 1604, King James I met representatives of the English Puritans at the Hampton Court Palace. After the meeting, which is known as the Hampton Court Conference, James authorised the translation of the Holy Bible into English, from the original Hebrew and Greek texts. The new bible is referred to as the King James Version.

✠ The Civil War

The conflict between the monarch and Parliament remained the central feature of the Stuart reign. Following in his father's footsteps, Charles I imposed taxes without Parliament's permission. This led to the English Civil War between the king and the arliament, lasting nearly a decade. The war was won by Parliament, with commanders such as Sir Thomas Fairfax and Oliver Cromwell. Charles I was charged with treason and 'other high crimes', and executed. The monarchy was abolished and a republican government, known as the Commonwealth of England, was established in its place.

After leading the parliamentarians to a decisive victory against Charles I and the royalists in 1648, Oliver Cromwell proclaimed himself lord protector of England, Scotland and Ireland

THE REIGN OF THE STUARTS IN ENGLAND

James I
1603-1625
Charles I
1625-1649
Charles II
1660-1685
James II
1685-1689
Mary II
1689-1694
William III
1689-1702
(joint sovereign with Mary II)
Anne
1702-1714

GEORGIAN ENGLAND

IN 1660, the monarchy was restored in England after a brief period of unrest. The Stuart Dynasty resumed its reign, with Charles II on the throne. Queen Anne was the last Stuart monarch. She died in 1714 and was succeeded by George I from the House of Hanover.

The Hanoverian coat of arms

George III spent his final years at Windsor Castle, due to his mental illness

The Hanoverians

The House of Hanover produced six monarchs, Queen Victoria being the last. Apart from Great Britain and Ireland, the Hanoverians also ruled Hanover in Germany. George I was the first Hanoverian king. Although George spent most of his time in England, he was more occupied with affairs of Hanover than of England. Besides, he could barely speak English. His son, George II, also gave preference to Hanover over England.

George III

George III ruled England for 60 years – the second longest reign in British history. His period is significant for the unification of Great Britain and Ireland to form the United Kingdom. Another very important event of the time was the Declaration of Independence of the United States in 1783. The English monarch was so against the independence of the American colonies that he even thought of giving up his throne.

The French connection

George III was a clever king who depended on efficient politicians, among them his prime minister, William Pitt the Younger. Pitt's tenure was marked by two events – the French Revolution that put an end to French monarchy, and the Napoleonic Wars that followed. The king eagerly supported Pitt's political and economic policies during the Napoleonic Wars. Napoleon's defeat at the hands of Horatio Nelson further improved the monarch's image.

It was during the reign of George III that Admiral Horatio Nelson, the famous British naval hero, defeated Napoleon at the Battle of Trafalgar

co[mm]issioned to compose four new anthems for the coronation. One of them is the well-known Zadok the Priest. The anthem has been sung at every coronation since then.

Tragic end

Towards the last years of his reign, George III became mentally ill and his son, the future King George IV, ruled on his behalf. It is now generally believed that the cause was a disorder that affected the entire nervous system. After spending about 10 years in Windsor Castle as a loner, George III died on January 29, 1820. By then he had become deaf, blind and completely mad.

William Pitt the Younger was the favourite prime minister of King George III. Pitt contributed a good deal in strengthening the office of the prime minister

THE HANOVERIANS' REIGN

George I
1714-1727
George II
1727-1760
George III
1760-1820
George IV
1820-1830
William IV
1830-1837
Victoria
1837-1901

QUEEN VICTORIA

A young Queen Victoria at her coronation. Britain became a dominant world power during her time on the throne

QUEEN Victoria was the longest-reigning English monarch ever. She ruled the United Kingdom of Great Britain and Ireland for nearly 64 years! By the end of her period, Britain had a vast empire and became the most powerful nation in the world.

✠ Accession

On June 20, 1837, King William IV died leaving his niece Victoria to succeed him. She was only 18 at the time. Being a woman, Victoria had no claim to the Hanover throne. For the first time since the Hanoverians came to power, England and Hanover had separate rulers. The young Victoria depended on her prime minister, Lord Melbourne, and her husband, Prince Albert, for advice.

The Royal Albert Hall in London was named after Prince Albert

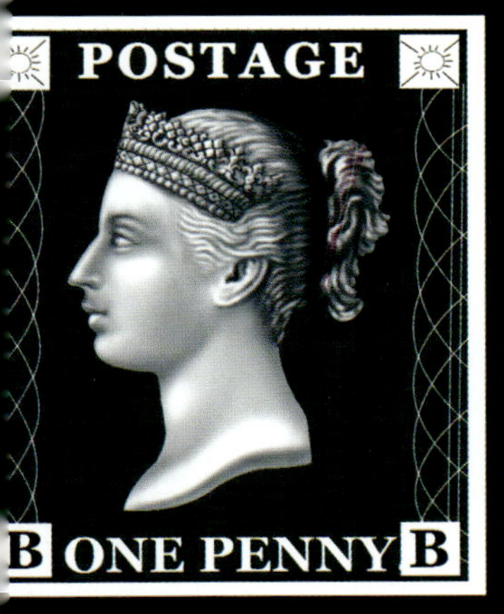

The Penny Black issued on May 1, 1840, was the first postage stamp in the world!

Progressive reign

Queen Victoria's reign witnessed several new inventions. In fact, she was the first reigning British monarch to travel by train. She was also the first monarch to be photographed and use a telephone. Postage stamps were also introduced during this period. The Penny Black, the first-ever postage stamp, had an image of the queen on it.

Irish Potato Famine

The Victorian Era was a prosperous one. However, one event nearly damaged all the good work the queen had done. It was the Great Potato Famine of Ireland. In 1845, Ireland was struck by a famine that lasted for over four years. The blight destroyed the main source of food for the Irish – potatoes. More than a million people died and about two million left the country.
The British government of the time was also blamed for the severe effect of the famine, on account of its economic policies. Some who held Victoria responsible named her the Famine Queen.

It was Prince Albert who popularised the Christmas tree in England. The tree was originally a part of the celebrations in Germany. When Albert married Victoria in 1840, he put up a tree at Windsor Castle. It was decorated with glass ornaments, candles and gingerbread. Soon, people across England were following suit.

A photograph of Queen Victoria and Prince Albert, along with their family, around the Christmas tree, was published in a newspaper. This made the tree popular throughout England

Born on
May 24, 1819
Ascended the throne on
June 20, 1837
Married on
February 10, 1840
Died
January 22, 1901

Widow of Windsor

In 1861, tragedy struck the queen. Her husband died, leaving the monarch devastated. She never fully recovered from this tragedy and wore black for the rest of her life. She withdrew into her castle and refused to make public appearances for a long time. This earned her the name Widow of Windsor.

THE BRITISH EMPIRE

A number of political decisions made during the time of Queen Victoria left a lasting effect on England. On numerous occasions the country also played peacemaker to prevent major wars.

✠ Reform acts

The Second Reform Act was one of the most significant achievements of the Victorian era. Passed in 1867, the bill increased the number of men who could vote. Several towns, previously not represented, could elect their members to Parliament. However, towns with a population of less than 10,000 had no Parliament member. The period was also marked by the growth of the two-party system that exists today.

✠ Conflicts abroad

The period also saw Britain take an active interest in issues abroad. In 1854 it became involved in the Crimean War. Britain supported the Ottoman Empire against Russia in the war. Victoria encouraged her troops by giving stirring speeches. After the war she introduced the Victoria Cross for valour. In 1857, the British East India Company faced a series of armed uprisings in India, called the Sepoy Mutiny. The rebellion was crushed. Thereon, the Crown decided to take over the governance of India to avoid future uprisings.

A map of the British Empire during Queen Victoria's reign. The red areas indicate the British colonies of the time

The Sepoy Mutiny of 1857-58 led to the end of the British East India Company's rule in India, and the establishment of the British raj that lasted nearly a century

The Victoria Cross continues to be the highest award for bravery in Britain

✠ Making peace

Following her husband's death, the queen showed an increasing preference for peace. In 1864, she urged the British government not to participate in the Prussia-Austria-Denmark war. In 1875, she wrote a letter to the German emperor, who was her daughter's father-in-law, helping prevent a second Franco-German war.

✠ Boer War

Towards the end of her reign, Britain once again became involved in an overseas conflict. This time it was the Boer War. Fought between the British and Dutch settlers in South Africa, the war had the queen's complete support. The war finally ended in May 1902, with the Treaty of Vereeniging. The treaty brought the Boer republics of Transvaal and the Orange Free State under the British Empire. During the war 78 Victoria Crosses were awarded to British soldiers.

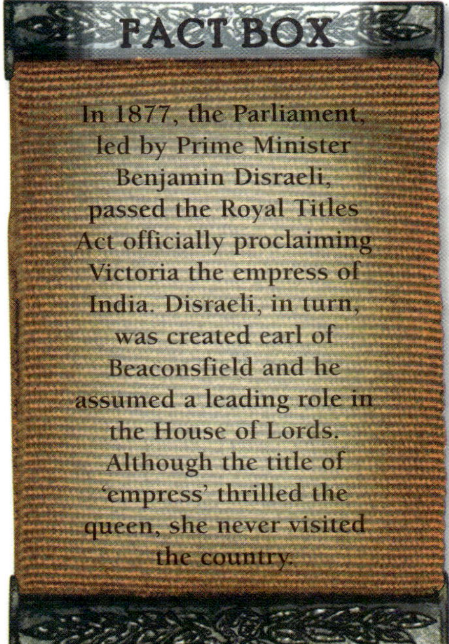

In 1877, the Parliament, led by Prime Minister Benjamin Disraeli, passed the Royal Titles Act officially proclaiming Victoria the empress of India. Disraeli, in turn, was created earl of Beaconsfield and he assumed a leading role in the House of Lords. Although the title of 'empress' thrilled the queen, she never visited the country.

PRIME MINISTERS DURING
QUEEN VICTORIA'S REIGN

William Lamb,
2nd Viscount Melbourne
Sir Robert Peel
Lord John Russell
Edward Smith-Stanley,
14th Earl of Derby
George Hamilton-Gordon,
4th Earl of Aberdeen
Benjamin Disraeli
William Ewart Gladstone
Robert Gascoyne-Cecil,
3rd Marquess of Salisbury

Australian soldiers at the Boer War. Australia was a British colony at the time and in those days, British colonies were forced to fight battles involving Britain

WINDSOR ENGLAND

KING Edward VII succeeded his mother Queen Victoria at the age of 59, having been heir apparent to the throne longer than anyone in British history. Edward was also the only monarch from the House of Saxe-Coburg-Gotha, which was later renamed the House of Windsor.

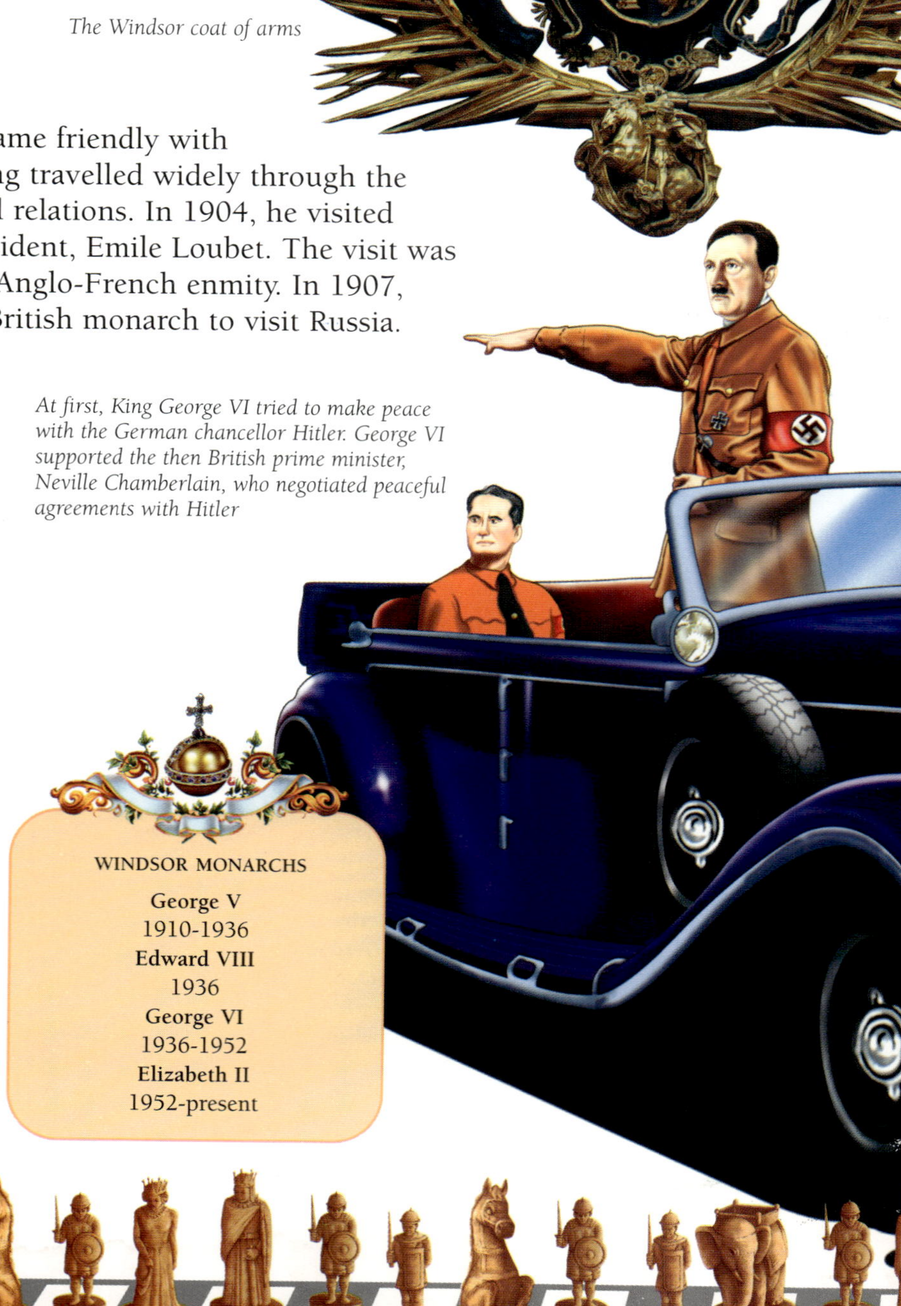

The Windsor coat of arms

Edward VII

During Edward's reign Britain became friendly with other European countries. The king travelled widely through the continent to improve international relations. In 1904, he visited France as guest of the French president, Emile Loubet. The visit was responsible for eventually ending Anglo-French enmity. In 1907, Edward VII also became the first British monarch to visit Russia.

World Wars

Edward was succeeded by his son George V. The new king's reign was marked by World War I. The war presented an especially delicate situation for the royal family because of its German and Russian connections. The German emperor Kaiser Wilhelm II was a cousin of King George V, who was also related to the Russian tsar Nicholas II – killed along with his family at the end of the war. In order to respect British sentiments, George gave up the use of any German title or style – and officially adopted Windsor as the surname for the living descendants of Queen Victoria.

At first, King George VI tried to make peace with the German chancellor Hitler. George VI supported the then British prime minister, Neville Chamberlain, who negotiated peaceful agreements with Hitler

WINDSOR MONARCHS

George V
1910-1936
Edward VIII
1936
George VI
1936-1952
Elizabeth II
1952-present

An Indian coin depicting George VI as both king of Great Britain and emperor of India

✠ All for love

After George V died, his son Edward VIII ascended the throne. Edward, however, ruled for only 325 days. The young king wanted to marry an American woman named Wallis Simpson. Mrs Simpson had been divorced twice before and hence was not considered worthy of becoming queen. On December 11, 1936, Edward announced his decision to give up the throne in order to marry the woman he loved. His brother, Prince Albert, Duke of York, succeeded him as King George VI.

✠ Unwilling successor

King George VI was not at all eager to become the king. It is said that he wept for hours in his mother's presence when he heard the news. Eventually, though, George VI proved to be one of the best-loved monarchs ever. He is most remembered for his brave decision to stay in London even after Buckingham Palace was repeatedly bombed during World War II. His reign also witnessed the decline of the British Empire, especially with India – the main British colony – becoming an independent nation.

Mahatma Gandhi, the famous Indian leader, played a crucial role in India's fight for freedom from the British Empire

THE LEGACY CONTINUES...

KING George VI was succeeded by his daughter Elizabeth II, who is presently queen of the United Kingdom of Great Britain and Northern Ireland. She is also commander in chief of the British Armed Forces as well as Supreme Governor of the Church of England.

A twenty-pound note with the image of Queen Elizabeth II

On April 9, 2005, Prince Charles married Camilla Parker Bowles, duchess of Cornwall, at a quiet ceremony

✠ Accession

In 1951, the health of King George VI began to fail. His eldest daughter Elizabeth stepped in to take care of her father's duties and made public appearances on his behalf. On February 6, 1952, the king died and Elizabeth took over. Her coronation took place on June 2, 1953. It is said that Elizabeth's grandfather, King George V, had wanted her to become queen one day.

✠ The reign

Elizabeth II married Prince Philip in 1947. They have four children. In recent years, the queen has undergone some difficult times due to her children, three of whom have had unhappy marriages. The failed marriage of Prince Charles and Princess Diana, in particular, affected the queen's public image.

British pop legend Elton John enthralled millions of people with his rendition of the song Candle in the Wind, *at Princess Diana's funeral*

✠ Prince Charles and Diana

The wedding of Prince Charles and Lady Diana Spencer was one of the most celebrated events in British history. Within no time, the new princess of Wales became an adored royal figure. The marriage, however, did not last. On August 28, 1996, after a much-publicised separation, Charles and Diana became divorced.

FACT BOX

Princess Elizabeth and her husband, Philip, Duke of Edinburgh, were in Kenya when they received the news of her father's death. Elizabeth was in a treetop hotel when she succeeded her father to the throne. Today, that hotel, where a princess became a queen, is a famous tourist destination.

After passing out of Eton College in Eton, at Berkshire, England, Prince William enrolled at the University of St Andrews, Fife, Scotland

QUEEN ELIZABETH II

Born on
April 21, 1926
Sister
Princess Margaret
(August 21, 1930-
February 9, 2002)
Married on
November 20, 1947
Husband
Prince Philip,
Duke of Edinburgh
Coronation
June 2, 1953

CHILDREN

Charles, Prince of Wales
(born November 14, 1948)
Anne, Princess Royal
(August 15, 1950)
Prince Andrew, Duke of York
(February 19, 1960)
Prince Edward, Earl of Wessex
(March 10, 1964)

✠ Prince of hearts

A year after her divorce, Diana was killed in a car crash in the Pont de l'Alma road tunnel in Paris, France. The news of her death was received with shock and grief all over the world. Her funeral was attended by about three million people and was watched by millions more on television. Diana and Charles had two sons, princes William and Harry. Prince William is the eldest and as such, the next in line to the throne after his father.

ROBES AND RICHES

THE royal family is represented by numerous symbols. Apart from rich clothes and jewellery, the royalty is also symbolised by coats of arms, flags and seals.

✠ Crown Jewels

The Crown Jewels have been used by various kings and queens since 1660, or perhaps earlier. They consist of the regalia and other state crowns, church and banqueting plates, robes, insignia and medals. The crown and other items used during the coronation are collectively known as the regalia. It is thought that Edward the Confessor was the first monarch to use a regalia.

Since 1303, the Crown Jewels have been kept at the Tower of London under high security

✠ The coronation

During the coronation at Westminster Abbey, the monarch is escorted to the Coronation Chair by a procession carrying the regalia. After the coronation oath, the Archbishop of Canterbury anoints the monarch with the ampulla – a golden eagle flask containing holy oil – and the spoon. The monarch then wears the coronation robes. The Golden Spurs, the jewelled Sword of Offering and the Armills are then presented. Next, the Sovereign's Orb is placed in the monarch's right hand, followed by the presentation of the coronation ring and sceptres.

Finally, the Archbishop of Canterbury places St Edward's Crown on the monarch's head.

In 1649, Oliver Cromwell had the regalia broken into pieces and sold off. The gold from the regalia was used to mint coins. Only the Coronation Chair was preserved

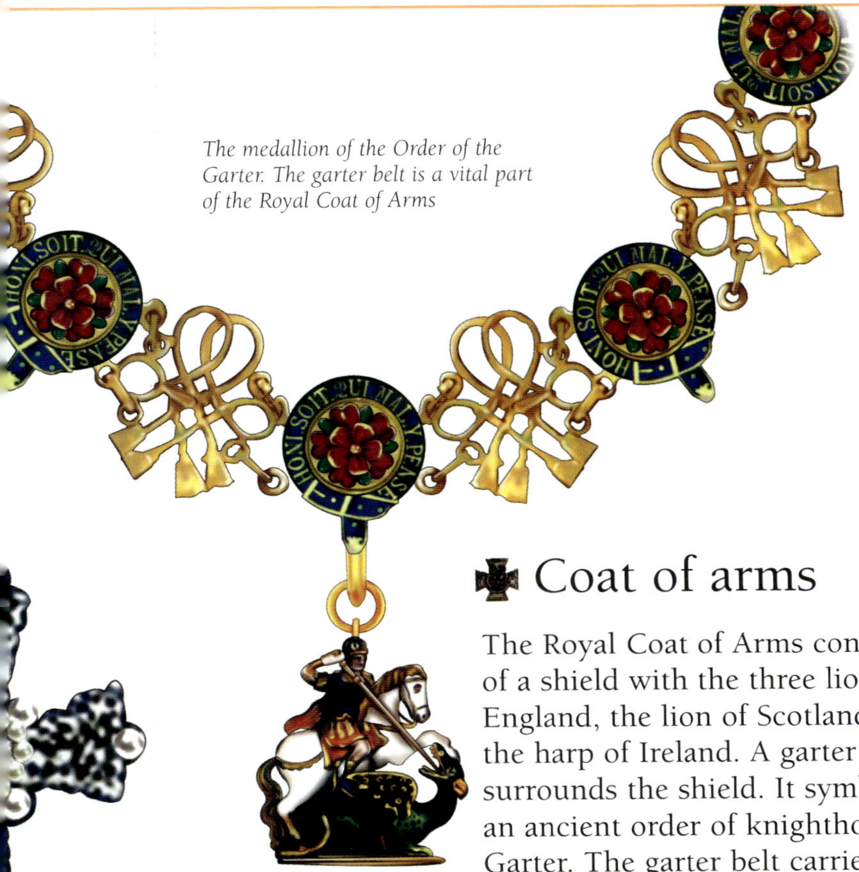

The medallion of the Order of the Garter. The garter belt is a vital part of the Royal Coat of Arms

The Sovereign's Orb was first made for the coronation of Charles II. The orb had precious stones and pearls, worth more than a thousand pounds!

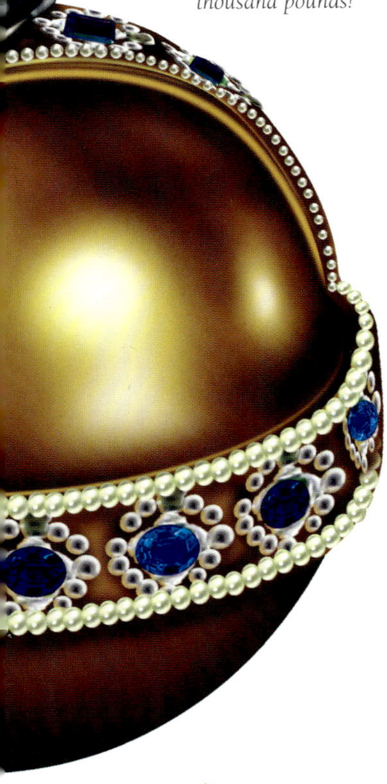

✠ Coat of arms

The Royal Coat of Arms consists of a shield with the three lions of England, the lion of Scotland, and the harp of Ireland. A garter belt surrounds the shield. It symbolises an ancient order of knighthood called the Order of the Garter. The garter belt carries the motto of the order, "Evil to him who evil thinks." The royal crown is mounted on the shield, which is supported by the English lion and the Scottish unicorn. The motto of the sovereign, "God and my right," appears below this. The rose, thistle and shamrock badges of the United Kingdom are usually displayed beneath the shield. The coat of arms of members of the royal family are similar to that of the queen, with just some minor differences.

✠ Royal seal and flags

The Great Seal of the Realm is used to show that the monarch approves a particular state document. The seal was first used during the reign of Edward the Confessor. The royal family uses several flags. The Union Jack, which is the flag of the United Kingdom, was originally a royal flag. The Royal Standard is flown on any of the royal palaces whenever the queen is staying there. It is also used on the royal car during official journeys, as well as on aircraft when stationary.

SIGNIFICANCE OF SOME OF THE REGALIA ITEMS

Three swords
Represent mercy, spiritual justice and temporal justice
The Great Sword of State
Symbolises the monarch's royal authority
Spurs
Represent knighthood and chivalry
Armills
Represent sincerity and wisdom
Sovereign's Orb
Represents Christian sovereignty
Coronation ring
Represents kingly dignity

ROYAL HOMES

The State Rooms of Buckingham Palace contain paintings by such great artists as Rembrandt and Rubens

THE royal residences are rich in history. Their architecture and interiors reflect the personalities of the various British monarchs who occupied them. The present homes of the royal family have been divided into official residences and private estates.

Statue of Queen Victoria at Windsor Castle

✠ Buckingham Palace

Buckingham Palace, the monarch's official London residence, is without doubt the most popular royal residence. The palace was originally a townhouse owned by the duke of Buckingham. King George III bought the house in 1761 for use as a family home. It was King George III who decided to convert the house to a royal palace, though it was Queen Victoria who first took up residence there (1837). Certain areas of the palace are open to the public on a regular basis.

✠ Windsor Castle

Windsor Castle is the largest occupied castle in the world. It has served as an official residence and fortress for over 900 years now. Originally built by William the Conqueror, the castle has been rebuilt and redecorated by his successors. Henry II rebuilt the Round Tower, the upper and lower wards, and the royal apartments in the upper ward, all in stone. Edward III built the majestic St George's Hall, while St George's Chapel was built during the times of Edward IV and Henry VIII. Ten British monarchs have been buried in the chapel.

Kensington Palace continues to be a private residence for several members of the royal family

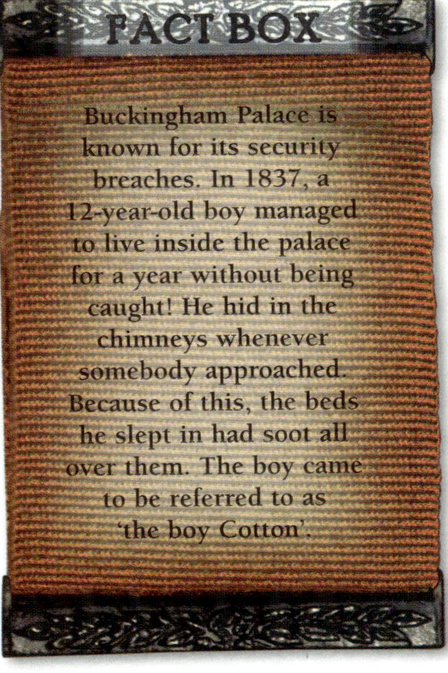

OTHER ROYAL RESIDENCES

Frogmore House
Palace of Holyroodhouse
Sandringham House
Clarence House
Kensington Palace
Tower of London
Hampton Court Palace
Palace of Whitehall

St James Palace

St James Palace is one of the oldest royal residences. It has been a royal residence for over 300 years. Built by Henry VIII, the palace has been witness to some of the most notable events in royal history. There it was that Queen Mary I signed the 1558 treaty surrendering the French province of Calais. Both Charles II and James II were born and baptised at St James. Also, some prominent royal weddings, including that of Queen Victoria and Prince Albert, took place there. Today, the palace is used for entertaining foreign dignitaries and as venue for other formal occasions.

Balmoral Castle

Balmoral Castle in Aberdeenshire, Scotland, was bought by Prince Albert for his wife, Queen Victoria. Both husband and wife had fallen in love with the scenic beauty of the Scottish Highlands. Prince Albert built a new castle near the old building, since he considered the original castle too small. Today, the Balmoral Castle is the holiday home of the British royalty.

The original Balmoral Castle was built during the 15th century

GLOSSARY

Abolish: End a particular custom, one that is especially unpleasant – like slavery

Adapt: To adjust or to embrace

Adorned: Decorated

Ascend: Climb, or rise

Banish: To drive someone away from a place, especially as a punishment

Baptism: A religious ceremony

Behead: To kill a person by cutting off his head

Blight: Disease in plants caused by fungi

Bog: Soft, wet ground, marsh

Cavalry: Soldiers who fight on horses

Claimant: A person who thinks that he/she is entitled (has a right) to something

Colonise: To take control of a particular region, or country

Conspirator: One who conspires

Conspire: Make a secret plan to commit a crime, or do someone harm

Coronation: The ceremony in which a person is crowned king or queen

Descendant: Child, grand child, nephew or niece

Dispute: Disagree, argue

Evident: Clear

Excommunicate: To bar from the church

Fief: A plot of land that has been let out to a noble

Garter belt: A belt worn around the thigh to hold up a stocking

Heir: A person who will inherit property or position of another when the latter dies

Heir apparent: Someone who has the highest chance of succeeding to the position of another

Hill-fort: Celtic roundhouse built on a slope, and surrounded by a ditch and a dyke to keep the enemies away

Insignia: A badge indicating a person's rank or position

Missionary: Someone, like a priest or nun, sent on a religious mission

Monarch: King or queen

Oust: Forcibly remove someone from a particular position

Outlaw: Criminal, bandit

Pledge: Promise, vow

Plot: Plan

Prominent: Important, noted, well known

Rear: Breed

Rebellion: To rebel, or oppose, fight against

Rebel: One who opposes

Reforms: Changes that bring about improvement or progress

Revert: Get back to, return

Revive: To bring back to life

Revolt: Oppose authority

Sacred: Pious, holy